THROUGH DROUGHT AND PETRICHOR

WORDS FROM MY HEART TO YOURS

ARMAN JASIM

For my parents who have showered me with unconditional love and support, Dr. Md. Jasimuddin and Dr. Kousar Jahan.

For my little ones, Khushi and Arshi

Contents

Contents

Foreword

From the first time I met Arman in the fourth grade, I knew he was going to be an inspiration for many like me. He had all the qualities of an intriguing writer. Every story he told in the boarding school dormitory with a torch in his hand was a performance, every poem he recited at the stage used to leave the audience in awe, and every time we parted ways he gave me a soul-warming hug accompanied by a gaze from those dreamy eyes. He embodied the gentleman image with class, charisma, and most importantly, genuineness. Today, as I write this foreword to his captivating collection of poetry, I assure you that every sentence that comes out of his ink will intrigue you, will make you ponder deeply and most importantly, will stay with you.

-Prateek Soumya

Preface

When the sun goes down, when the rain pours straight on your conscience, when the night never seems to end and when the heart yearns for a reason to keep beating, it is in those moments that I sit by the sweet scent of petrichor of the rain that keeps pouring through my eyes and write.

And that universal emotion which sometimes pours as rain and sometimes as words on my diary is precisely the reason why i believe that my readers are always connected to me, through drought and petrichor.

1. The Girl in White

It was a cold winter afternoon
The sun was clearly out of sight
Just as she drove past in her car
I could just see a glimpse of white

A white sweater, sleeves pulled over her palm
She got off in a keyed up hurry with a bag on her arm
She hustled towards the class leaving me bewildered
Bewitching me as she left behind a memory so calm

I see her again, walking on the sidewalk
Its evening but I haven't had a talk
Anxiety always gets the best of me
And I'm scared of stuttering on just small-talk

I wish to discuss Harry Potter
And all the books she has read
I wish to discuss philosophy
Whether God's actually dead?

And then discuss if Freud was a madman
Or was he a genius in disguise
And then pull a joke on Oedipus complex

I mean who would even fantasize?

But as I daydream of her, night falls by
And I don't even turn to say good-bye
But anxiety, my old friend never leaves me alone
So I stay with the old friend
And watch the girl in white go home.

2. Time

If you take a video of a frame with a passing rover
Speed it up to infinity while you play it over and over
The car disappears but the frame remains
Isn't that car just a prisoner of time's restraints?

Infact aren't we all just mere seconds of the clock
Caged in an hourglass, losing sand from the stock
Who knows tomorrow, where the dunes might flow
The more I learn, the more I don't know.

My body will be as obsolete as the hourglass
When I meet the One who happens to surpass
Everything that exists; I see Him and I see me
Existing through time indefinitely.

3. The Unexpressed

My eyes are almost an ocean
my chest burns with fire
it lights up to push me over
towards a never-ending desire
Like the sun caged in clouds
waiting to burst as rain
As an unresolved yearning
of a delightful pain
My eyes, they smile
and my tears constrained
Even a touch from a loved one
leaves this feeling untamed
A feeling so fierce and intense
yet so compressed
sobs between the walls
of the unexpressed.

4. Read Your Poems To Me

Read your poems to me
bring me back to life
For there is something in your literature
that makes the dead in me alive.
So the breeze that you write about
can find its way to me
And the fire that you brood around
can light up the dead in me.
Don't touch my hands before
your poetry thinks of them as summer rain
Don't touch my soul before
you write of what you've felt of my veiled pain.
I want you to write me letters
like the good old days
with crushed flowers within
Darling, you know the ways.
And I will be waiting always
Just like a lover from the good old days.

5. The Girl in Headscarf

She hides behind her headscarf
A dozen thoughts that are compelling
Her to say this and do that
They're always talking and telling

Things that don't exist
Scenarios that'll never come by
But they get so loud sometimes
That she has to listen and comply

"Am I presenting myself well?
Am I being too much?
Am I resenting them again
By blabbering too much?

''Maybe I should just keep quiet
But wait, what if that's rude?
I don't like this EDM on the speakers
But will they get mad if i play 'Hey Jude'?"

Hush! I want to shoo them for her
For once I want her to adjust her scarf
I'll look down while she does that

I want her to put those thoughts afar

Because she's beautiful the way she exists
And nobody gets to say otherwise
Not even the voices in her head
Because they don't see what people see in her eyes.

6. Love by The Cafe

To fall in love is to not know someone
because there is something about secrecy
Like the way I find myself at an odd cafe
watching her stir sugar in her warm coffee.
To fall in love is to have never spoken
because we hope that eyes might speak
But to my misery, her's speak French
And i barely know past *croissant et la steak.*
To fall in love is to be confused
at the moment when they smile at you
To love is to walk past them in the hallway
Just to find a glance or two.
I wish she'd shoo off the butterflies
I wish she'd break the ice
But every morning she's gone
before I can sip off my coffee
before I can finish off the croissant slice.

7. The Trichotomy of Thoughts

I have an ocean in my possession
Yet a drop is what I seek
This poem is more of a confession
Of a landscape that turned bleak

A trichotomy lives within me
Forever existing as a dissonance
Three screams echo within me
As I lose my sanity and sense

One demands a pleasurable destruction
Surpassing all bounds and belief
The other seeks an equilibrium
But finds itself in grief

The former hurts the latter
Over and over again
The latter addresses the matter
But all is drowned in vain

The silence within me is deafening
Almost as quiet as a cloud

That's struck by a blinding lightening
Waiting for a thunder that loud

I wish they'd merge within a shadow
The lightening, cloud and the thunder
Id, Ego and Super-ego
The trichotomy is where my thoughts surrender.

8. Man in The Mirror

I look in the mirror and there he stands
Its all the same from toe to hands
I've always wanted to talk to him
But between us, remember the mirror stands?

I have his aggression, I carry the same guilt
Despite it all, such a fine man he has built
Because his love is also what I've inherited
Though, his company, it was always limited.

He kissed my little hands and bid me goodbye
A ten year old at boarding school would always wonder why
It was my decision too but how did it all get so hard
That I had to cross days on the calendar and cry.

At the price of not seeing the cocoon turn into a butterfly
At the price of not being able to sing me a lullaby
He had a lot more to lose now that i realise
I never doubt the importance of his decisions and the goodbye.

Now when I look in the mirror, he looks older and tired
But the compassion in him, *mashallah* never retired

So the butterfly is flying a path that he led me on
To bring him flying colours of yellow that he has always desired.

9. Two Fruits

Two fruits on a lonely tree
One forbidden and the other's from heaven
I wonder what made them so different
Probably the sun or maybe the crescent

The tree strives to keep them ripe
Yet not all could grow the same and thrive
It sighs at its destiny and calls upon the skies
To keep them both growing, to keep them both alive

The roots, they haven't moved in decades
Just grown for the sake of both fruits
The one that stayed near got the best
The one at the edge fell from the shoots

"But there are seeds within you"
She tells to the falling fruit
"That one day you'll shoot up from dust
And germinate your own roots."

"Soon, the other fruit shall follow" she says
"And under the earth, we will entwine in ways
Growing is a process that takes time and days

So be adamant to put whatever it takes."

The tree is my mother, my sister's the other fruit
I'm the one that woefully fell off the shoot
But I'll listen to her 'cause she's the only solace
Hoping on the other fruit to cheerfully follow suit.

10. Different Pages

Everytime I catch a glimpse of her
And whenever we share a smile
Memories linger on as scribblings
And words that I fail to compile

I write because she compells me
By the way she rocks her chair
I write because she tells me
A lot through her stare

We haven't exchanged much words
But she's the reason why the ink keeps going
But how do I finish this poem
Without taking to her, without knowing?

If Wordsworth was alive, he'd forget the daffodil
If God was alive, he'd lose his own free-will
And they'd all write sonnets and verses for her
But they still wouldn't do justice to my muse, whatsoever

My poetry longs for its muse and it has been ages
Since the walls around me have kept me in cages
Because I don't want to lose what I've never had

Probably we'll be in the same book but in different pages.

11. The Veiled Hurricane

In a bittersweet melancholy
I find myself in the arms of another
Walking past a summer of regrets
Waiting for the winter to get her.
Just as a granger wishes for downpour
I wish for this woman in September rain
And as John Green would put it
"*I was drizzle and she was a hurricane.*"
Quite literally, she seems fidgety
Guess she passes on the anxiety
But I like all of it, the whole of it
An intoxication, I can't explain in soberity
She speaks so much but tells so less
She's a lot like me, sorted but a mess
She's building walls around her, I wonder why?
But for this woman, I'm climbing nevertheless
The walls are like the veil she hides behind
And I'm waiting for a spring when I can finally climb
Leaving behind an autumn of fallen leaves and sins
Waiting to be consumed by the hurricane and the winds.

12. A Paper Poem

Inspired by John Green's Paper Town and Margo Roth Spiegelman

sOmeTiMes yoU've gOt to tAkE tHe cLiMb just to fAll
sOmeTiMes yoU've gOt to aVeNge aNd cAuSe a bRawL
aLL I'm saYing is yOu've gOt to tHink oUt of tHe bOx
'cAuSe "iF YoU dOn'T imAGine, nOtHiNG haPpEnS aT aLL"

sOmeTiMes yoU've gOt to sAy soMe ciaos
sOmeTiMes yoU've gOt to bReAk deAd vOws
aLL I'm saYing is wHen tHerE's nO guARenteeD tOmoRroW
dO wHatEvEr mAkES yOu hAppY 'cAuSe "*Forever is composed of nows.*"

tHeRe's A fiNE liNE bETwEEn loVe aNd oBsESsiOn
tHe fOrMer mAkEs yOu betTEr, lAttEr wOuLd wOrsEn
"*wHaT a tReChErOus tHinG iT iS*
tO bELieVe tHaT a pErSoN iS mOrE tHaN a pErSon."

yOu hAve aN uRgE to eScaPe bUt yOu fiND yOur rOotS

cUrLeD
iNto sOmEtHiNg tHat'S cLoSe to yOu bUt sEeMs aBsUrD
"*iT iS sO hArD to leAve — unTil yOu leAve.*
aNd tHeN iT iS tHe eAsIest gOddAmneD tHinG iN tHe wOrlD."

bUt bEfOrE I LeAve, I hAvE tO dO a lOt
"bEcAuSe tHe tOwn is pAper,
tHe mEmOriEs aRe nOt."

13. Labyrinth

I was stuck in a tunnel
Every day was a night
Being lost in a labyrinth
I was losing my sight

When I ran out of water
I put poison down my vein
Until it clogged my heart
And putrified my brain

I had forgotten the colour of of skies
While I was surrounded by the blues
With such a diminishing sight
Wrongs over right I'd choose

Until that one day when I found two friends
One was will and the other was hope
In my heart, i kept them close
And decided, with them I'd elope

As we saw a beam of moonlight
My sight went hazy with a soul-stirring delight
I could barely see a silhouette of white

It was her who stood at the end of the plight

But standing under a silvery moon
I'm scared to hold her hand so soon
I wish to sing a song to her
But I'm scared that on harmonies, I'd go off-tune

Only when the poison runs out of my soul
I think, by the stars, I'd take her for a stroll
And if none of this makes sense to her
I'd fall back to the labyrinth and let it take control.

14. Resistance

Humans, we're all made of particles of biology
And we're prisoners of our own existence
Caged within the bounds of primitive urges
We've never cared enough to realise a resistance

A resistance to our own conditioned mind
To search if there's more than just livin' and dyin'
If there's more than pain and pleasure combined
If there's more than two bodies illogically intertwined

Humans, we've all become unconditionally obliged
To norms that the creator built to control the mind
Oxytocin from touch, serotonin from drugs
Endorphins from cigerettes that control your guts

A control that we hand over to external triggers
Imagine if you could control these chemical figures
Don't just imagine, rethink about the resistance
Rough road, dispiriting distance but at the end, you define your existence.

15. Little Things

Sitting at the corner of my room
My gaze traces the raindrops
As they race down my glass pane
This is where life stops.

Oh! The trance of little things
What a misfortune to have not noticed
The aroma of the coffee my friend brewed
The love of the ones closest.

I stand up to pick up a book
My gaze flips through the pages
Oh! What a bliss it is
That I had missed upon since ages.

Its still pouring and I feel like humming a rhyme
So I pick up the ukulele and strum my favourite line
Oh! The ecstasy of little things
Like singing Lana Del Rey's "Summer Wine".

Strawberries, cherries and an angel's kiss in spring
My finger on the second fret strumming A minor on the string

No more am I scared of melodies that i can't hum
Whatever octave it is, I'm throwing my hat in the ring.

The rain stops as silver shines through the glass
I observe how it sees seasons but never shatters
The love of little things, as I'm bringing to pass
I realised, I am that little thing which matters.

16. Swimming to The Shore

I'm unbothered when they don't understand me
Or refer to me as a weird clown
Because those with waterlogged lungs
Just wish to see others drown

Those who gave up hopes to swim
Made homes in a drowning dystopia
And I'm least bothered to tell them
There's a lot more to the world, if not utopia

They talk behind my back
Assuming that walls don't have ears
How funny of them to assume
That the ones who've had my back don't hear

But I'm glad I have people
Who wish to see me live
The universe laid this rule
That you get what you give

Now that I have the energy
I'm swimming towards the shores

Far away from the drowning sailors
Soon to get back to old chores.

17. Because You've Loved It

When the sun casts its hue over the skies
I sip coffee around the grass and smile
Its odd that I wait for the orange-yellow skies
And when the night falls, I wait for the fireflies.

I look up for hours to wish upon a falling star
And wish that you wish what i wish
But if you don't, then I look for another star
And wish for this longing to perish.

Because longing hurts in a beautiful way
But this beauty is somewhat tragic
What if I stopped longing for you one day
The stars, the moon, they'll all get static.

I've read hundreds of pages to know you a little
I've looked up your favourite song and hummed it
That makes me question myself,
How often have I loved a thing because you've loved it?

18. The Girl in Red

Odds have never been in my favour
I've always liked things I can't have
Like the pink candy, probably peach flavour
When I was ten, ten pennies is all I'd have

But I'd never settle for a popsicle for ten
I'd wait until I'd have a hundred
But things are complicated way more than at ten
Now I ask myself, should I still wait for the girl in red?

I've also liked rainbows once
I've obliviously chased after the horizon
I'd never settle for a single nuance
If I hold a dream, there's no compromisin'

So I'm still looking for the pot where the colour starts
And I'm waiting for the girl in red, the muse of my arts
But only if destiny wills to destine me a destination
It surely won't just move one, but both hearts.

19. Candy

She's all the colours that appeal a painter,
She's like the apricity of a noon in mid-winter,
As Perry would put it *Thinking of You*
"*She's like a hard candy with a surprise center.*"

A charm that draws me in an inexpressible insanity
Whenever she passes by the streets in my vicinity
Why do I see things now, that have always been?
I know it is destiny giving me signs of synchronity.

I wish to give her sunflowers,
I wish to buy her a drink,
But i also believe that
I need some time to think.

To think that what is meant to be will be,
But if I'm chasing her,
Won't she be running away from me?
If she's a candy all soft and sweet,
Does she deserve the innocence of a sweet-tooth,
Or will she just rot my sensitive teeth?

20. Jacob's Creek

I'm not sober enough to stay in my wits
So I'll write about you in pieces and bits
I still know, for God's sake how thin and narrow
Are the chances of you reading this tomorrow

But in the charm of *Jacob's Creek*
My inhibitions are probably tired and weak
So I'll write about how your hazel hair
Frizzes through my thoughts in this autumn air

And I'll write about your eyes
And the poetry they speak
On your lashes, I realise
There's always a prose exquisitely unique

You aren't just a drunk thought
You're infact the intoxication
And I'm buzzed before I gulp a quart
Because admiration stays unlike infatuation.

21. Consequences

I make homes by the meadows
And guard them with wooden fences
Then I break them with my own hands
Thinking of sheer expenses

The broken windows yearn in despair
For a presence, for a silhouette to be there
Yet you and I walk the same path
Leaving the home by the meadows back there

What could have been, couldn't be
Because we were busy being what we should be
But in a world that merely exists because of uncertainty
Could it have been more than what it could ever be?

Now that's another uncertainty
Unconcerned of miniscule thoughts of humanity
What might seem like a sane behaviour to community
To me, is nothing more than a conditioned behaviour of insanity

Tell me if I turn back in a hundred years or so
Would I find you lingering by the fences

Would you then live, not by conditioning
And not caring about the consequences?

22. A House Between The Walls

A house between the walls insurmountable
Yearns for a dweller to knock at the door
The one who feels hiraeth inexpressible
Someone who would walk on this floor

The house doesn't long for limerence
It is just better when someone dwells
One who would read by wooden fence
The stories of fallen kingdoms and realms

The walls that were built after they built the house
Till date manages to cage it in an oblivion never-ending
The solitude infact protects the house
But keeps it from ever befriending

Because the house doesn't see it
That it is always the walls that take the fall
Until they scratch it from within
Burn the doors and break the wall

The house is my heart
The walls they're all concrete

This time, I've locked the door
Enduringly waiting for them to find the key.

23. Poetic Disguise

Have you ever swallowed a lump of pain
When you're sitting by your friends and fumes,
When you try to talk but you can't explain
A feeling that is evanescently lost in brumes?

Have you ever felt a pain in your neck
Like a glaive is grooved along your throat,
When you're sitting by a dense deck
Realising you don't belong on your boat.

Have you ever sat by the moon
Realising how close it is yet so far?
Have you ever felt people fade away
On a starry night like a diminishing star?

Have you ever felt an urge to describe
Your bottled blues in a poetic disguise?
Because people they make sense to me
And on odd days not at all.
Perhaps because they're are like seasons,
After a spring, they fade away with the fall.

24. The Opthalmologist

She sits by the ophthalmoscope
She sees through his eyes
That he's been hiding from the world
A vision that beholds beautiful skies

She asks him the read the Snellen
He reads L D P H N
But he doesn't read her mind saying
I L Y S M

The Jaeger he's fluent at
but he can't read between the lines
Sadly she writes 6/5 on the prescription
For a person who is apparently blind.

25. Inertia

Its been a while since I've felt your presence
But not a thing in me has changed
Apart from the tarnished silver presents
That I've still kept on your desk arranged

You must be out there somewhere
Floating without a definite gravity
While I'm still falling in here
In a reality made out of irrationality

They ask me to stop mourning
They teach me time's linearity
But how do I wake up every morning
Without my only ever known family?

They say you moved on the day you left
But every movement is subjective to a frame of reference
You're somewhere out there looking at what you left
A man caged in inertia, forever reminiscing in your reverence.

26. Mirror

I see him in the mirror
He's different at every stare
From the last time I saw him
His skin is tanned, he's losing his hair

He stares back at my soul
Like he's wanting to be caressed
But how do I love someone
I can't look at undressed

He's got stretch marks all over his hips
His chest is sagging like an arc
So I turn off the lights and cry with him
'Cause i can't see him in the dark

When it's half past twelve, he tells me
A hundred tears he's shed
To keep my heart keep beating
To love me when I sob in bed

He asks me to turn the lamp on
I see his skin dipped in Darjeeling tea
And his frizzy hair like Medusa's

Tell stories of birth, death and the infinity

Naked, his hips have ripples like in a painting
Of a pond whose vision my soul has been wanting
His chest breathes in particles of an infinite cosmos
I wonder how so much was hidden right under my nose

A soul and a body falling in love
"You're enough", he says "You're enough!"
"What you see in the mirror, the novel view,
Its less of me and more of what's within you!"

27. Only Woman I've Ever Loved

She was intimidating like the only flower that bloomed
In a deserted garden, with a silvery light of the moon
The only woman who I've ever wanted to be touched
By, The only woman I've ever loved

Her hands fit mine like flowers in a corsage
A lot of my personality comes from her panache
The only woman who never bought me a drink but got me buzzed
The only woman I've ever loved

She was strict on the outside with a heart so tender
She was like a warm blanket in a windy winter
She's walked through my heart and left it scuffed
The only woman I've ever loved

She's now a vine of flowers, blossoming on her own
Had I still been by the garden, nature's order I'd have torn
Now my heart is like the moon, the craters she's scuffed
The only woman I've ever loved.

28. Yearning Heart

My lips have always had another to kiss
Its just my heart that yearns for another
To be kissed just reminds me of ephemerality
To be loved is what it seeks forever

My body has rubbed another irrationally
Its just my heart that yearns a gentle touch
Being with bodies that feel hollow and empty
My heart years for a lot but not much

I'm present in a moment
I'll zone out in another
Amidst a world of rocks
I seek a love like feather

Hither and thither on lonely rivers
Sailing on a cold night with freezing shivers
My hands get cold steering the boat
They seek a unison only and only with hers.

29. Platonicity is Dead

I like the way she speaks
I like the way she dresses
I like the way he keeps
A track of my progresses

I love her taste in music
I love his hands on the guitar
But complimenting them is quite tragic
When humanity from humans has been quite afar

So I never tell her how amazing she sounds
Because I know she'll think I'm hitting on her
And I never tell him that I love him
Because I know a different story he'll stir

I text them paragraphs only to be left on seen
Basic human interaction has lost a lot between
A confusion that i don't blame them entirely for
Todays society in the dreads of dystopia has laid these norms.

Where friendships weep over a frustration
Of being caged into boxes of complexity
The hands of hypersexualisation

Have throttled the existence of platonicity.

30. The Letter

You alone were my fate
I'd have done anything for you
For without you, I'd still be jade
Like an old withered clock with a cuckoo

One that was held in the constraints of time
One that demanded a mere look
One that would cry by the hands of time
Like a dusky damaged book

One that nobody cared to read
For the cover they precisely judged
But you surprisingly disagreed
And at once I felt loved

Loved, like a book that's put to chest
Loved like a scent that stirrs unrest
Loved like a wish that I leave to manifest
With this letter that conveys the unexpressed.

- Connect with me on Instagram- @arman.jasim
- Connect with me on Spotify- Arman Jasim

ARMAN JASIM

9 798887 335339

Printed by Libri Plureos GmbH in Hamburg, Germany